T0194276

CYNTHOLOGY

A Collection of Rhymes
Book III – **Shades of Cyn**

Cynthia Young

authorHOUSE®

AuthorHouse™
1663 Liberty Drive
Bloomington, IN 47403
www.authorhouse.com
Phone: 1 (800) 839-8640

Published by AuthorHouse 06/07/2016

ISBN: 978-1-5246-1276-4 (sc)
ISBN: 978-1-5246-1275-7 (e)

Library of Congress Control Number :2016909145

Print information available on the last page.

Any people depicted in stock imagery provided by Thinkstock are models,
and such images are being used for illustrative purposes only.
Certain stock imagery © Thinkstock.

This book is printed on acid-free paper.

Because of the dynamic nature of the Internet, any web addresses or links contained in
this book may have changed since publication and may no longer be valid. The views
expressed in this work are solely those of the author and do not necessarily reflect the
views of the publisher, and the publisher hereby disclaims any responsibility for them.

First paperback edition

For information about special discounts for bulk purchases,
please contact Cynthia Young, at www.cyoungbooks.com

Available in E-Book and Soft Copy at www.authorhouse.com

Cover design by Shutterstock©

Contents

Cynthology A Collection of Rhymes

Reader Favorites

Introduction

I have been a caregiver since 2002. I wrote **Memoirs of a Caregiver** to tell my story. While I was writing this book, I felt the weight of many years of love, tears, frustration and grief. I wrote my first rhyme for my aunt's funeral service. After that, it seemed as though they were always in my head. Writing them down became a much needed diversion from everything else I had going on and it became my escape. I finally decided to publish them as **Cynthology A Collection of Rhymes** which depicted my view of life.

I was inspired by my readers' to continue to write and a second book of (unedited) rhymes evolved. **Cynthology A Collection of Rhymes Book II-Electrified** is a compilation of original rhymes.

Readers' range from 18 to 80 and are touched by the rhymes on subjects they are familiar with and relate to. **Cynthology A Collection of Rhymes Book III-Shades of Cyn** also has original rhymes that speak to past and modern day issues and common situations that people deal with frequently. These rhymes are not *nursery school* rhymes and depict mature subject matter for the grown and sexy.

I want to connect you to real life situations through my poetry that are relatable and understandable. I hope you find these rhymes to be thought provoking, inspirational, uplifting, even shocking, leaving you with a message to ponder.

Once again, please enjoy the rhymes and find your favorites from this collection too.

Enjoy!

Cynthia Young

My thanks, love and gratitude to my family, friends and readers'
Who continue to encourage and support me

Cynthology

Cynthology is my view of life
From being a kid in a good neighborhood
To becoming a wife

Life is good, bad or indifferent
I've been to the school of
Hard knocks and bumps
Believe me, I've paid my
Dues and handled my lumps

Love, happiness, loved ones loss
I dealt with many until
They went home to the big Boss

I have good friends, known many
Men and stuck with the good one
That put a ring on it in the end

Now it's my time to shine
Drink some wine and dine
Drive the road and see what
I dream about

I'm finally free to be me and I want to
Shout it out!

A Nod to My Past

This is a nod to my past, some of it unclear, some of it
Rekindles my fears, gone are those days I'll never
Bring back

As I sit in my room listening to songs that are relevant to
My life, I remember friends that went on their way and the
Boyfriends I didn't keep, over these I certainly will not weep

Things happened that I can not change and they will
Forever remain the same

I miss those I can no longer touch, damn I miss them so very
Very much

I will remember times of joy and happiness with family and
Friends gone to glory and they will always be
A part of my story

Life goes on and I am living proof of that, I can't linger in my
Grief and sorrow because those that are living want me back

There were misunderstandings and decisions that helped
Shape my world and made me the person I am today

If my old house could talk, it would sigh and keep my secrets
In the walls until the end of time

I love the music from my past; the music that played in the
Background of my life as I became a daughter
Friend, mother and wife

I am grateful for experiences that gave me life long lessons
I was smart enough to use

So, as I live in the now with a nod to my past, I know
This very day won't last; because it's already in the past

After the Show

After the show, the girls line-up outside the stage door
Dressed to kill in booty shorts and high heels, their
Weaves are flowing and their eyes are glowing

The competition is fierce - not a trick is missed to
Catch the performer's eye. She desperately wants to
Make him her guy

She wants the thrill of being with him, to brag
About her sexcapades with her girls at the gym
After all he's a big star, she might even keep
His sperm in a jar

He sees the cast of characters and makes his move
He picks the one with the long dread locs and
It's off to the hotel so she can rock his jock

Now that she's with him she starts to change her mind
She doesn't know if she wants to take the ride

Deep down inside, she comes to realize that she's not
The kind of freak he wants, he insists that she have
A drink to calm her nerves

The next thing she knows she's sitting on the curb
Disheveled and bruised, she called the cops and
Went to the news

Date raped and humiliated, she's embarrassed for people
To know that she stood outside the stage door

She really thought she wanted to go with him; but soon
Found out the hard way, that he did **not** respect
Her right to say **NO!**

Ageless Love

He knew he would love her from the first time
They met and he vowed to love her always
On that you can place your bets

She raised his children and shielded him from
Any attack; she is the kind of woman
That always has her man's back

They struggled together, communicated and
Weathered their storms, in this day and
Age that's not always the norm

She treats him like a King but is not subservient
To him for anything, she knows her worth and
Strides beside him on any turf

When women come at him he rejects their advances
For he knows he already has his gem and
He will not jeopardize her love for them

Beautiful inside and out she carries herself
With style, grace and a whole lot of class
She's sexy and knows how to make him
Love all of her sass

Not one to be crossed he knows she's really
The boss and that's just fine with him
He is happy to be in her life and that is why
He did not hesitate to make her his wife

A man with a woman like this knows he needs to be
Truthful, faithful, compassionate and have a listening ear
He needs to be gentle, loving, attentive and above
All respectful

As you grow old she will be ageless and the love
She has for you is all you will ever see

Be a man that handles your business and keeps his
Wife out of harms way and she'll love you always
Until your last day

Assaulted

I am assaulted by the memories of your touch and
Your beautiful smile that I love so much

I am assaulted every time I walk past your door and
Realize that you are not there anymore

Years of memories linger in my heart and mind and yet
I can not find the comfort that I need

An assault comes every day, all day, I must stay on
The move to keep them at bay

If there is anything I know, it's how much I love you so
I am under attack by my inability to bring you back
For selfishly I didn't want you to go

The thoughts in my head are scrambled and confused
I stumble from room to room looking for a way
To cope

Each day that passes brings hope that the assaults will
Lessen and I can go about my day without your
Memories getting in the way

Only time will help me loosen my hold, break these
Assaults and allow me to put my precious memories
Of you away in a vault

Never fear, I will forever keep you near, for you
Have touched me like no other, for I am and will
Always be your Mother

Authentic

I struggled with the thoughts and images in my head
That ran loose; as a young child, I knew something
About me was different even though my mother
Named me Bruce

I'm uncomfortable when I must act like a boy and
I feel like a girl, I love the way I look with dresses and
High heels on, that really should be my world

Years go by and I have lived the lie to please my
Family and friends, to save them from the embarrassment
And the shame they would claim if I were to wear lipstick
Paint my nails and change my name

I will no longer live a lie, all my life I lived as someone
Other than my authentic self, now I will trade that life
And put the old one on the shelf

I am finally part of a new life with friends that relate
To me, I am freer than I ever thought I could be. I have
So much to learn and I'm willing to take the journey

Try to remember, even though I am different on the outside
Over time, I hope you will come to see; that my heart and
Soul has not changed and is still a part of me

Accept me for who I am, be happy for me, for I am
Truly blessed to be able to live two separate lives in
One lifetime

Now, that I have decided to be my authentic self
I pray you will appreciate the long journey I took
To become who I've always wanted to be

I made my decisions before it was too late
I stand before you reborn and I am proud to
Introduce you to my authentic self ......

Hello, my name is Cait!

Awakening

So many troubling thoughts are in my head that they woke
Me from my dreams

I arose in the darkness of night and roamed through the
House that was quiet and serene

As I stood in the window looking into the night, gradually
The sky opened and let through new light that painted
The clouds in purple, pink and orange
It was truly a beautiful sight

The light calmed my fears and made me see rainbows
In my tears

With the new light of day I'm looking forward to
Finding answers to the questions that fill my
Head and keep me from resting peacefully
In my bed

When I get in my own way I always falter
That is why on this beautiful morning
I will cast away my worries and leave
Them on the alter

Renewed hope surges within me and I know that
No weapon will prosper that is formed
Against me

The Universe will guide my journey through
The peaks and valleys of life and take me to
Wherever I am meant to be

Nightfall will come again and I will seek
Refuge in my dreams this time resting
Peacefully

Binding Ties

Have you ever loved someone so intensely that your
Heartbeat quickens, the words in your mouth seem to
Thicken and you just can't think straight?

Loving hard, giving your all you never notice that there
Is no reciprocation and the relationship begins to stall

But, you move ahead as your family and friends watch with
Dread knowing that you are not using your head

You think *"what do they know, they don't understand that the
Sex is so good it overshadows my pain"*

The hurtful words, put downs and attempts at making you
Feel ashamed, you can't do anything right and that always
Seems to bring on a fight

What's it going to take to bring you to your senses? You still
Fall under his spell when his name is mentioned

Finally, the pain overcomes the pleasure, you realize that after all
The years of yearning for his touch, the touch you loved so much
That you don't need him the way you thought; because you
Are worth much more, something your family and friends
Told you many years before

After years of built up tears your head is clear, now you know that
He covered up his lies and shaded your eyes, by giving you many
Nights of good loving between your thighs; but when it's all
Said and done it wasn't enough and you finally found the
Strength and the will to break his binding ties

Black Sugar

They called her Black Sugar down on the farm, she
Walked barefoot through the fields alone, daydreaming
Kicking rocks and swinging her arms

She wanted to play with the other kids, but they laughed at her
Calling her black and ugly; those words hurt her feelings and
Made her cry

She vowed she would show them one day that she
Was beautiful too and she left the farm with
A long lists of things to do

Education was first, she graduated from law school
Number one in her class and avoided the men
That wanted to touch her ass

Yes, she was sexy and had a body that men dreamed about
But her mind was the treasure that the right men sought

Black Sugar returned to the farm, with a twenty carat
Ring on her finger and a very rich man on her arm

The ones she left behind didn't get away, they stayed
On the farm working hard in the fields every day

Much to her hater's surprise and dismay she's the one they
Look to for their pay; because she owns the farm and
Everything they can see for miles around

Who's laughing now she thought to herself "*I'm still black
But I'm not ugly anymore, I'm the one that
Came back and settled the damn score*"

Bladey Mae

I've been calling and texting you day after day
Month after month with not much in the
Way of a response

You know I work hard for my money and
That ain't no joke, I'm the only one in my
House carrying the yoke and right now
I am as mad as I can be

I helped you out with your emergency even
Though it was not an urgent matter for me
My patience is gone, you better get real and
Pick up the phone

Mixing money and friendship is never good
All the excuses on why you haven't paid me
Just make me want to kick your ass through the hood

And please, tell me how you have the nerve to be
Mad at me for asking about *my* damn money

I have to let you know in harsher tones that you will not
Get away without paying back my coins, you should know
By now I'm really not the one

Your promises to pay with your tax refund check is
As Judge Mathis would say; really whack. Why do
You think I would even believe that!

Before you wear that brand new suit or
Make a payment on that Escalade

Just remember, my name is Bladey Mae and
I'm the one with the nine-inch switch blade!

Blind Eyes

He sees her on the stage and he listens intently
To what she has to say; as she has become all the rage

He can not believe how she has stirred his physical and
Mental emotions and he longs to touch her, some way
Somehow, he has to touch her

Their eyes meet and sparks fly, he knows she's older
But he has blind eyes, for she is beautiful to him
In all her womanhood, when she touches
Him it's all good

He wants to know her thoughts and dreams, he wants
To learn from her in every way, he wants to love her
And he does

When he touches her it's no surprise; her skin is smooth as silk
He knows she thinks his breath still smells like baby's milk
But, she let him touch her and he doesn't want to stop

She lets him get on top and from there she teaches him the best
Way to rock. He is in shock over all the things he didn't know

She is agile, tireless; her age never shows. His hands
Caress her breast. She reaches between his legs, and
Strokes and strokes, then glides down on him, he can't
Hold back, he violently erupts to her experienced touch

He Is lost in her womanhood and he doesn't
Want to stop

She tries to push him away; to find someone else. Oh, no
She is all the rage, he has turned blind eyes to her age and
She is who he wants, he'll always love her for the
Rest of his days

For she has taught him valuable lessons he will never forget
Through her, he has become a man, he has learned from her
To love and not just have sex

He wants her and he will be with her for the rest of their
Lives, for she is all the rage in his blind eyes

Bully Within

She was over weight again…..
She walked by mirrors so fast her image was a blur
She didn't see what other people saw in her…..

Some say, that she has a pretty smile, warm heart and
Is generous to a fault, with lots of passion for her art

She remembered being fat shamed when she was
Young and the words of the hater's stung and hung on

Every time she gained weight, she bullied herself
With self-hate

She shied away from photographs and looked at
Them with a discerning eye; because in her mind
Pictures didn't lie

She had to dig deep to stop the bully within
She allowed it to take away her pride and steal her joy
Way too long

Working hard to kill the harsh thoughts in her head
She fought through her body image issues and
Came out strong

When she looks in the mirror now she see's her confidence
Self-control, self-pride, self-esteem and a woman that has
Learned to love herself inside and out

But the most important thing, was driving the bully out and
Learning to shut-down the hater's and her own self-doubt

Butt Crack

He walks down the street cool and slow
That's really as fast as he can go
He walks like a penguin his pants are so low

His pants are belted around his thighs
Underwear showing, butt crack too
He graces you with that bad luck when he
Walks away from you

He constantly grabs his crotch, just saying
What's up with that?
Maybe he's checking to see if his junk
Is still laying where he touched it last

With his feet pointed side to side he waddles
His way to his destination, hoping to stay
Out of sight, in the night, afraid the police
Will ride down on him and he'll have to fight

If that happens they'll hook him up on GP
'cause in this neighborhood if you don't look
GQ that's exactly what they do

Even that thought doesn't deter him from
Walking down the street, cool and slow
Underwear showing, butt crack feeling
The breeze

He keeps his hands on his jeans trying to
Look cool; but he's really holding on
So he won't fall to his knees and
Look like a damn fool

Church Lady

Sunday morning she is up and ready to be seen
In her very best outfit and hat, she is dressed
To the nines, she has the new Preacher on her mind

She plays a big role in the church, she tells the young
Girls not to let the boys put their hands up their skirts

She flaunts her position in the church and looks down
On others that really do all the work

She touts her virtues all over town, she lays her
Hand on the Bible and talks about supporting
Her fellow man; but does nothing to help
Even though she can

Monday morning, she leads a different life, she
Regresses to short skirts and hitting the club for
A drink or two, she turns away and pretends
She didn't see you

Her faces are similar; but not the same, she plays the
Holier than thou game, then gossips about you behind
Your back and hatefully calls you out of your name

She spouts verse after verse from the Bible; but Monday and
All through the week, she's pulling a flask out of her purse
Get in her way and she damn sure will curse

On Sunday she starts all over again, sitting in the front pew
Watching the Preacher from under her hat brim
All the time scheming on how she can get with him

Church lady, is what she pretends to be; but take it from me
This chick is hell on wheels running around fake as can be
There's probably a few like her in your midst
Keep your eyes open so you can see

Cold Dark Night

Lola and Lana were loving sister's getting along and
Making plans; until Lola met a handsome man

Lana couldn't hide her disdain, for she thought he
Should be her man

The sister's separate with nothing in common anymore
Because Lola caught her man red handed with his
Hands in Lana's pants in her bedroom on the floor

The man said *"Don't trip baby, I've got enough for both
Of you, your sister can show you what I like to do"*
Lana said *"I love him and he loves me. I'll do whatever
He wants, unlike you; you're too busy going to church"*

Lola cried and couldn't seem to dry her eyes
In the quiet of night, she heard a voice that told her
*"Dry your eyes and don't let them play you
I'm going to tell you exactly what to do!"*

Every man has a weakness; so Lola went to work
She was determined to show her sister this man was
Nothing but a low down dirty jerk

Lana had no idea what she would find when she entered
The dark damp room, she heard mumbling and finally
Found the light; only to find her man holding his manhood
In his hand, he was a bloody sight

As it turned out, Lana's man had been with a real
Pretty Transvestite and when he found out she wasn't
A *real* woman they began to fight

Oh well, looks like he lost that fight, because half of
His manhood is laying somewhere out there, in the
Cold dark night

Lana finally realized that the guy was nothing but a jerk and
This time, he put his hand under the wrong damn skirt!

Combat!

Every day in some way we are subject to go
Through combat

We combat illness, weight loss, financial woes, bullies and
The depression that comes with losing a loved one

You strive to combat the trials and tribulations that come with
Living – you must overcome them because your work
Is not done and you seek purpose in your life

In other words fight the good fight every day, when life
Throws you curve balls, mean streaks, kicks in the ass and
Tough breaks - bow your head, kneel and pray

Combat the urge
To give up! To give in! And never say no!
Because N O just means the next opportunity is
Coming your way

Death of a Friendship

Many phone calls are made over many days with no response
The ones that are don't make sense

The friend waits to see what happens next with the ball in her court
Waiting is hard and brings the breath to her lungs a little short

Growing up so close they kept each others secrets, wiped each
Other's tears and celebrated their successes over many years

One made her way to glamour and fame, while the other one
Worked tirelessly to get attention for her name

Tragedy strikes from out of the blue and the fame that was known
Loses its luster and turns its back on her
Her world spins out of control

Her friend's step-up but are eventually
Turned away, she doesn't want
Them in her life; she wants to stand alone in her strife

So no phone calls are answered, no text messages returned
Assistance is refused and it becomes clear, she no longer
Cherishes the people she once said were dear

She initiated the death of their friendship and hasn't looked back
Her friend finally realized that people
Come into your life for different
Reasons or seasons and she made peace with her friend's decision
To step out of her life

Deuces!

As I reminisce on our break up, I know now why our love did not last
It's just another day to ponder our past and I think....

How I long to send you my usual text, I long to hear your voice
Not just in my head and I long to have you near me in bed

We use to fit like a glove, but you changed and began to withhold
The things I held dear, you were hard to live with, hard to love
What happened to us?

Your passive aggressive behavior and mean spirit
Made it easy for me to leave

No more tender touches that I loved so much, no more
Mid-day calls to laugh and talk and no more long walks

I couldn't live with you, now I'm without you, remembering
Your habits that got on my nerves and things you refused
To do for me that was significant in my world

It's hard to hear a song that we danced to and played when
We made love

Making love with you was pure joy, all I do now is lay
In bed and use my toys, squeezing my eyes shut so I can
Pretend you are with me, inside me, holding me

Yes, I'm alone but not lonely, I will survive and it may be
Hard tor awhile but sniveling and crying for a long time
Un-huh, not my style

The fastest way for me to get over you, is to get under
Someone new; believe me I will not sit at home alone
Like a sad little doll on a shelf

Recapturing my stifled dreams, my self-esteem and
Self-worth is more important to me, than what I thought
I needed from you. You took me to school, thanks for that
From now on I won't be anybody's fool and I won't look back

Deuces Baby, I'm back on track!

Do You Know Me?

We've been together for a very long time and I wonder
Whether or not you know the things I value
Inside my mind

Do you know my heart and how I want it to be loved and
How you still make it flutter like the wings of a dove?

Take your time and look deep into my eyes and I assure you
There won't be a surprise, just the things you should know
That will make you love me even more

Do you know me well enough that you can tell me
What I'm about to say?

Yes, is the answer to my questions, you've
Shown me many times through your actions

When you open the door, pull out my chair and
Glide your fingers through my hair

Your gentle kisses on my cheek, the way you love me
Between the silk sheets

Letting me sleep late to finish my dream, then
Bringing me fresh brewed coffee with lots of cream

These are the things you do to show me that
You know me very well and the feelings inside
Me that you evoke, I will never let another quell

Dog to Dog

She was a sweet young innocent thing when she met
The man of her dreams

He broke her heart so she moved on to other things. She views
Men through shades of blue always thinking they'll
Cheat on you

Men are called Dogs in the romantic world
When they break a woman's
Heart with mean harsh words

They're known as Cheater's without a conscious
Nothing matters to them when all they're thinking about is
How to fill their tip to the rim

Dogs lick and scratch themselves and trot through the neighborhood
Looking for a bitch to hump

Men are no different, they have plenty of issues and they're out
Looking for a woman who will take their dump

Lessons learned from the men in her life taught her to think
Live and have sex the way they do

Make it quick down and dirty, just get in do the do and don't
Let anyone get their hooks in you

She is a beast in the bed and she gets inside their heads, her sex is
So good it makes them want to jump off the roof

She tells them upfront *"When you come at me and try to flirt*
You better come correct, or you'll find out quickly that
I am a Pit Bull in a skirt!"

Dog Tags

Dedicated to my dad
Sunset 11/07/14

A young man, barely eighteen years of age
Is drafted, given dog tags and sent off to war

Fighting the hostile weather, marching
Toward the enemy he was sent to kill
Never knowing from one day to the next
If it would be his last, he drew upon all his
Survival skills

Every letter from home was a very big deal
They helped him keep his head in the game and he
Prayed for a safe return to home cooked meals

Never again having a desire to roam, the dog tags
Were put away, his prayers were answered he was
Fortunate to be home

He lived a good life with his daughter and wife
Working hard to take care of them

After he passed away, the dog tags were taken from
The drawer, his daughter clutched them to her heart

For that is where they laid when he wore them
So many years before

With the dog tags close to her heart, she feels his
Presence around her

Knowing that his blood runs through her veins
She is proud to carry on in his name

Dreams Come True

The day is hot and sticky and she's moving slow
She wished for cooler weather but now she knows
The Zebra striped leggings, pink satin shirt, lime green
Scarf and high heel shoes with no heel tips, scraping the
Sidewalk is going to make her feel worse

People point and stare at her matted blonde synthetic hair
Her body jiggles when she moves, she clutches her tattered
Worn empty purse under her arm, as the sun beats
Down on her face

She asks strangers for nickels and dimes and they look
At her like she's committing a crime. All she really wants
Is a warm smile, a kind word and place to lay her head
It's been years since she's slept in a clean, soft bed

Rummaging through trash bins, picking out plastic
Bottles and cans is how she survives and every
Now and then she finds something in there
That's really worth her time

As she goes along her way, singing beautiful songs
Her voice is heard by a young man that makes her
Dreams come true. She becomes a star
On something called *You Tube*

Now, she wears a new dress every day and
There are no more meals from the trash, she
Sings for her supper and her pocketbook is
Full of cash

31

Eleven Years

We had eleven years of trials and
Tribulations and lots of fun
He chose our anniversary to tell me
He was done, he didn't want me anymore and
I was not the one. He abandoned me

I am filled with grief and I am not getting
Any relief, my mind doesn't stop and reminds
Me of all the things we did together in our house

No matter who is at fault I must move on too
I must pull my strength from the Universe. I must
Make sure from now on to take care of me first

I'm realizing that if you love someone and they
Want to go free, let them go. I know eventually
There will be someone better out there for me

Eleven years – I cried my tears, reminisced about all
Those years, wiped my face, drew in a deep breath
And now I'm ready to face my fears, clean the slate
And embrace what's to come in future years

I'll take my time and unwind, rewind, drink some wine
And re-discover me. It's time for me, to love me, more than
I loved him

Eventually this too shall pass. I'm growing stronger
Every day and I refuse to be bitter; because I know the
Love of my life is on his way

Faces of Cyn

Many thoughts run through my head
I create from anywhere, even lying in bed

I never know where the thoughts will go
Or where they might come from to
Give me words to write on a page and
Speak at a show

Erotic, poetic, inspirational, funny and
Thought provoking, I write the way
I feel and my thoughts are always about
Being real

They reflect the experiences of others
And my own sex appeal

I show my faces through the rhymes I write
And I love entertaining you with them
Night after night

The laughter and applause coming from you
Gives much happiness to the faces of Cyn too

So, it's because of you that I will continue to
Do what I do

False Promises

You looked good on the outside and showed up
To my door in a brand new ride

There was never a shortage of conversation
And you made a lot of promises

I believed you and waited for the things you
Said you wanted me to have; but nothing
You talked about ever came to pass

All I got was one disappointment after the
Other and nothing seemed to work out
For you and I

You promised to love me and take care of me
Instead you constantly disrespected me

I won't fall prey to your false promises again
You hurt me and you never admitted to
Doing me wrong

I picked myself up by my boot straps and
I have moved on

Thanks to you I am **Super Woman** strong!

Finding Myself

I am twisted and paralyzed, so I anesthetize myself
With food and drink, sitting in a chair, feeling
Confused and alone unable to think

People are all around me for awhile. Eventually
They move on and leave me to my grief
I am alone sitting in the chair with no relief

My grief poured out of my tears and did nothing to
Soothe and quell the fear that I would never overcome
My grief and living with it would take the rest
Of my years

You told me in a dream *"Don't grieve for me, set me free*
My time on earth is done. Celebrate my life, not
Death that eventually comes to everyone"

I sought a higher being in the Universe; I began to
Slowly, very slowly reverse day by day and when
I finally opened my eyes and cleared my head
I had returned to life and you still were not in your room
In bed

So, I focused on finding myself again and I will
Celebrate you with all of my being. I will keep you
Near and dear to my heart until I am with you
Once again

Flawed

No one is perfect, we all have flaws that we
Live with every day

Some people refuse to believe that they are
Flawed, in any way

How arrogant and selfish are they
To try and push that concept on
Anyone else

The put downs, the snide remarks that try and
Make another feel less

Who are these people that love to point
Out your imperfections, yet they
Can't see their own

Why? Because they're too busy tooting
Their own horns

As far as they're concerned they can do
It all, my question is this ....

Will one of those other people be there to help
Them up when they stumble and fall?

Maybe not, because this was the person
That said they could do it all

Forbidden

Her waist long golden blonde hair and blazing green eyes
Made people stop and stare

When she walked down the street a black man was
Required to look away and stare down at his feet
If not, he would be hung from the nearest tree

Forbidden love was in the air, black girls
Were summoned to the master's room
He had his way any time he felt like it
On a hot sweaty Georgia afternoon

Years go by and what has been forbidden
Begins to surface; but opposition still
Lingers as black and white conceal their love

Crosses burned and white sheets rode through
The night, causing a black man to take flight
Or lose his life

Golden blonde hair and blazing green eyes
Make men of all races swoon, she's the one
He wants to take to his room

She is who they covet and use as the standard for
Other women around the world

Black, brown, red, yellow or paper bag tan
Women of color are beautiful in their own right

Men take off the blinders and see how beautiful
The rest of us are in all of our glory and might

Fresh

She reads magazines that show what celebrities do and she
Wants to wear make-up, short skirts and high heel shoes
She's anxious to be grown so she can leave home

Watching a XXX rated movie with her boyfriend, has
Them staring at naked bodies having all kinds of sex

Fascinated and curious, she thinks she's in the know
But, she quickly finds out that she's no match for him
He took her virginity under the bleachers in the gym

Her parents are appalled that their little girl fell from
Grace and now her big belly is staring them in the face

Every day she hears her mother saying "I told you to
Keep your dress down and your legs crossed."

No longer the fresh faced, big eyed, innocent girl
Her parent's kicked her out. With nowhere to go
She stepped into another world

A world of darkness, strange men and paid for sex
She is the epitome of no longer being fresh

All she ever wanted was to be accepted and run with
The popular girls in her class, now they are laughing
At her because she's selling her ass

Her baby face won't last under the pressure to perform. She
Has a quota to meet and if she doesn't she'll surely get beat

A man lifted her up and away from the streets, he told her
She could be anything and everything she wanted to be

She's proud and triumphant now; she graduated from the school of
Hard knocks and bumps, survived her lumps and dodged the chumps

So who's laughing now!?

Ghetto Fabulous

Sharp as a tack, you'll never catch this girl in gym shoes
Or flats

Red bottom heels line the shelves in her closet and she
Is always up on the latest fashion

But, the landlord is knocking on the door, the rent is behind
Oh well, she had to have that pretty dress
By Anne Kline

She ignores the phone and the messages left behind. The
Bank is looking for her car again, she couldn't resist
Hanging out in the newest club with her friends

Yassss, honey she is ghetto fabulous! She has beautiful
Clothes and a face full of expensive make-up
She looks the part for any occasion
From the time she wakes up

Living paycheck to paycheck does not faze this girl
Her head is completely in another world, there is
No back-up plan, no 401K, she chooses to leave that
In the future, she has no time to think about old age

Over extended in every way, she lives to shop in
Saks Fifth Avenue another day, no matter that she is
Fashion poor, she wants to look good walking out the door

Even when the Sheriff is putting her fabulous belongings
Out on the curb, all she wants to talk about is buying
Something else she really can't afford

What's wrong with her? Young and dumb…..
Now that she's homeless; she'll be a well dressed
Ghetto fabulous bum

Golden Nights

Twilight is approaching and this begins her day
Day that is really night, she will work until daylight

She hesitates to linger in bed as she prepares for what
Lies ahead, black silk stockings grace her long shapely legs
Her lingerie is very classy; but always with a side of trashy

He arrives right on time and everything is ready
The lights are low, the music is on and the
Gorgeous view of city lights can be seen
From every room of her home

She hands him a drink and he whispers soft words
She knows his preference and strips him down
He knows what to expect from this beautiful woman
He knows she's been around

Naked as he can be, she stands over him and lets go of a
Golden stream, she talks real dirty and he is
Satisfied….. even gratified

He never wants to go inside her, he likes to
Watch as the golden shower pours down from
Between her thighs, he watches until he is blinded
By the pee getting in his eyes

As he dresses to leave, he tells her he'll see her
Tomorrow, for this ritual is a daily routine

She is paid a grip of coin for this specialty service
That is why, she can live in a penthouse and
Drive a Bentley all over town

Giving him a golden shower every night is
Easy money she would be crazy to turn down

Her Truth

A little girl grows up to be a beautiful young woman. That
Beautiful young woman turns into a nymphomaniac
Looking for a good time in the sack

Man or woman it really doesn't matter, she constantly
Listens to the chatter in her head that makes her
Determined to get someone in her bed

Years of having sex have gone by, she settles down with
The woman of her dreams; things couldn't be better
It seems this is what her life has come to mean

One day she falls back to habits from the past
She wants to do whatever it takes to
Share her ass

Her sexual frustration is off the chain, her woman
Doesn't do it for her anymore she's craving a man

A man that drives deep into her pent up desires; a
Man to bring her to heights she's known and missed
A man with chest hair and a great big d**k

She wants to go wild, have sex any time of the day
Anywhere, anyway she can, she has to shake
Her sexual frustration with a man

He plays it rough, she can take every inch, she's
Just that tough, she'll ride his wave of white
Flow until it is dust, she knows how to really
Tap out a guy

Sexual frustration brought havoc into her life, but the enjoyment
Of release with a man is how she feeds her true desire

Deep inside she knows *this* to be her truth and
She no longer wants to be a liar!

Hindsight

We were college sweethearts, nothing and
No one could pull us apart

During our summer break, my boyfriend
Asked me to come home with him to his families
House on the lake

I was excited and filled with joy, I wanted to
Spend every waking hour with this boy

When I got there his Dad greeted us at the door
My mouth fell open, how could this be, he was
The spitting image of his son and this
Was a surprise to me

I had never seen a Dad that looked like him
With flat abs, big muscles and a little waist
It was obvious he spent a lot of time
In the gym

Awww, man! I couldn't sleep that night, because
My boyfriend's Dad was giving me looks that burned
Into my flesh and made me feel warm and wet

I certainly never had those feeling for my boyfriend
He hadn't even tapped me out yet

The next day, the Dad stepped in my pathway, stroked
My hair, and rubbed my breast, I shouldn't kiss him
I didn't dare

But, Dad had other ideas; he took my hand and placed
It on the bulge behind his zipper, what I felt there was
Huge and bound to be a ripper

After that, it was on and popping, we had mad sex that
Night and the boy I thought I wanted.......Well, he just
Became hindsight

Hit the Breeze

The sun is out, your spirits are high
There are no clouds in the sky

Let the top back and roll the windows down
Hit the road, free your mind and
Let your worries go

Hit the breeze and let your hair down to flow
A ride down Highway One is what you need
As you watch the sunset and feel
The ocean breeze

Feeling fine, no worries on your mind
You can tackle the world refreshed

Go on, hit the breeze and show the world
Your very best!

Honey Trap

She worked the pole, she twerked her ass and the men
Threw down plenty of cash

She went through a gauntlet of men every night, they
Offered her everything from exotic cars to Hollywood fame and
Trips to islands on private planes

She wanted the one she couldn't have. He wasn't easily impressed
He stood in the shadows watching each night as she
Got on stage and undressed

Then one night from the shadows he emerged and
Grabbed her by the arm, right away she knew he
Wasn't there for harm

His embrace was strong, he grabbed her ass and
Kissed her hard with lots of tongue

Turning around she touched her toes and backed up against
His crotch, he pushed her g-string aside, took her from
Behind and had one long tumultuous ride

She invited him to play in the mud and that was a blast
It was his first time tapping out an ass

Her honey was sweet and something he longed to eat
Sixty-nine made their loving complete

Each night they performed the same routine, he was good
Real good at working that thing

The first time she danced in his lap he knew he wanted her
And now he's caught up in her honey trap

Hurry Home

They talked on the telephone while he was at work, he was
Stressed out, he said his boss was acting like a jerk

She told him not to stress, come to the parking lot and
See her new red dress

When he got to the car she did not disappoint him. Her dress was
Off the shoulder and skin tight, his hands began to roam

She kissed him with her luscious ruby red lips and slowly
Moved her hips, bumping, grinding and pressing his limits

His hands moved all over her body, down her smooth bare
Legs, up her thigh and there he found a pleasant surprise

His woman was naked under that dress and he could
Feel himself begin to de-stress

He eased his fingers inside her and she was wet, hot and
Throbbing just like him

When he felt her release, he removed his fingers and slowly licked
Her honey one finger at a time, they kissed passionately and
The things she was doing to him swirled in his mind

She stroked him and stroked him until he was hard and straight up
Then she kissed and massaged his head until it blew up

He wanted to continue their grind and he sure as hell
Didn't want to stay behind

I Know

With a sly smile, she whispered in his ear, *"This is just a tease to
Let you know, I'll be waiting for you with a surprise when you walk
Through the door"*

He hurried home with lust on his mind, her taste lingering on
His tongue and what do you think he found, that blew his mind?

His boyfriend on top of his woman working a sixty-nine

I Know

We have been together for a very long time, we even
Finish each others sentences and read each others minds

I know you love me because you tell me so in your
Gentle touch, the way you hold me when I fall asleep in
Your arms and you bring me beautiful flowers and
Gold charms

Spooning in bed takes our love to another level, it's not all
About sex all the time, it's how you caress me and
Develop my mind

I know I am everything to you because you never impose
Restrictions on me by censoring my words or putting
A stop to my shopping sprees and I am
Completely free to be me

I know that you and I are here to uplift and support
One another; not push each other down to make
One of us look bad while the other one
Takes the crown

Little pats on my butt as I pass you by, a kiss on the
Forehead and a wink of your eye, are things that
Uplift my heart and soul

You know I am your ride or die for there is nothing
I wouldn't do for you and you have shown me
That you love me the same way too and that is why
I know

I Touched His Heart

He put his hands on my body and gently, tenderly
Stroked me

It was so sensual, so loving and so exciting to feel the heat
Of his breath on my neck

The feeling of his warm tongue made its way down my chest
Along my belly and into the depths of my love and
That is where he finally came to rest

Right there is where I simmered while he evoked feelings
I have never had before and he opened the door for
So much more joy

Love me, oh Lover, love me, like it's our last time
Tell me, show me, hold me; take your time
While you travel along the curves and angles
Of my body sending shockwaves through my mind

Each stroke took me to another level, am I still in
This world or is this heaven?

We were building toward an awesome climax
But, while I was yelling his name, with my
Legs up in the air, I had to let out several
Really stinky farts

He didn't miss a beat and he still succeeded In
Taking our climax off the charts

That's when I knew he had true love for me and
I had really touched his heart

Indelible Kisses

His kisses are soft and supple and when he kisses me
The fine hairs on my arms stand up and I am
Transported to another place

His kiss caresses and awakens the erogenous zones
On my body and soft moist kisses adorn my face

Kiss me baby, kiss me slow and I will definitely
Let you know, that I am emitting my best flavor

His lips know where I like them to go
Kiss me slowly

I love the tongue within his kiss
Flicking and swirling it's nothing but
Pure bliss

Tongue me, kiss me, lick me, and suck …. my neck
Tomorrow, I know the hickies will show
I don't care, I'll wear them proudly and
Everyone will know

His kisses make me wet, as his tongue
Skims over my body, I begin to sweat

I crave those kisses, I think about
Them touching me throughout my day

I let out soft moans of pleasure when his kisses
Wash over me, kiss me baby and don't let it
Be the last time

I want another kiss, I'm craving the bliss
Slower, slower, that's it, Oh! Right there!
I feel release, as I wind my hands through his hair

I would trade my soul and give up my last dime
For his kisses leave an indelible impression
On my heart, soul, body and mind

Labels

When people look at me I wonder if they see a label on
My forehead that they think defines me

Black, White, Brown, Red, Fat, Skinny, Disabled, Short
Gay, Female, Nerd, Whore and so many more

Look past these labels and find out who I am and
How I choose to live my life

Am I a widowed wife, has there been tragedy in my life
Is there a reason for the way I act, have I lost many things
I can not get back?

You see me homeless by the side of the road, tattered and
Torn, worn, wrinkled and looking forlorn, what is my
Story, everyone has one

If you see a label, try not to judge, read the message in my eyes
That's the place my true feelings really reside

Take the time to delve inside and learn who I
Really am and you just may find that your goals and
Aspirations are the same as mine

Lashes and Lipstick

Lashes and lipstick are applied, extensions are
Added to the hair, the fragrance
Of perfume lingers in the air

The dress is high above the knees and sure
To please. Now, it's time to hit the breeze

The club is bumping the music thumping
It's time to dance and find romance

Kissing and rubbing makes lust bubble up
They sex in the bathroom stall and on his
Knees he aims to please

He turns around
For his partner to do the deed, it doesn't
Take long; he loves to do it with speed

The fun continues throughout the night
He finds two others and they slide out of
Sight, it continues all night long

He's having so much fun he doesn't want
To go home, as he stumbles down the
Stairs he's barely able to stay on his feet

Trouble has followed him down the street
Three bullies push him into a dark alley
They have their folly and this time
It's not fun, for they are rough and
Mean and leave him in a bloody stream

Lashes are askew and the lipstick is smeared
The five o'clock shadow is showing his beard
He lies on a stainless steel table with a sheet
Covering his face

His father always told him wearing lashes and
Lipstick was a sin and would bring him
To this very end

Linger

I am mesmerized by your beautiful brown eyes and I am
Engulfed in the depth of love that I see in them and I can't
Look away, so I linger there every day

As I kiss your soft full lips your mouth parts and my lips cling
To yours, just a bit longer and I linger

Your body has all the right curves and I swoon at the thought
Of touching you, my hands enjoy the ride down your spine
Across your butt and inside your thighs

Sweeping you into my arms and holding you I don't want
To let you go, we make love for hours and I know
While I'm inside you, I will linger

Your magnetic pull is undeniable, irresistible and I just
Want to be where you are; loving you with all of my might
Long into the night

When I run my fingers through your hair, relax, close
Your eyes and I will rock you gently to sleep and
Place warm kisses upon your cheek

While I watch you sleeping in my arms I will count
My blessings, for you are *everything* I want and
You will always linger in my heart

Madam

The Madam has been around the block more than once
She's been with Pimps since she was a teen still in jeans

Now, she has a stable of her own, she never liked
Working for anyone, she couldn't wait to be on her own

With sixteen girls and two guys working for her
She can not deny, she likes things the way they are
She wears fabulous furs and drives big fancy cars

She knows what the girls have to do, she was once
One of them too, when tricks get out of hand
She takes care of her own, she smacks
The trouble down, laughs her ass off
And has another glass of rum

Every now and then, she throws her hat back in
The ring, she puts on sexy lingerie and gets to work

The Madam is the best at her trade, she lets the man
Rub his hands up her legs

She's wearing crotch less panties and his fingers
Roam to find her sweet spot, he'll have no trouble
She is very hot

He enjoys the pleasures she knows how to bring
She'll get a huge tip for doing these things
Using her hand up and down his tool
She straddles him and he goes inside
She's still got it, she'll take him for a
Hell of a ride

He breaks out in a sweat and slaps her on the ass
She stretches out along his body and pumps him
Up and down, round and round and side to side, until
They end up in a pool of stickiness with him
Still inside, he's not through he's waiting
For another ride

Man Down

Walking to her car after a hard days work, she looked
Forward to going home, a hot bath, putting on something
Cool and sheer while she lounged and watched
Her favorite programs with a cold beer

Her thoughts were interrupted by a shadowy figure who
Came at her with a knife and threatened her life

She calmly tried to talk to him but he was jumpy and
Waving the knife in her direction, she knew he was high
On something and he wasn't listening

Suddenly, he lunged at her and grabbed for her purse
She stepped to the side, grabbed him and threw him to
The ground

Before he knew what was happening
He was in a triple chokehold securely bound

Man down!

His face was beet red, his eyes bulged in his head and
He was gasping for air as he tried to pull at her hair

He was no match for this seasoned MMA fighter and
He had no clue about all the things she was able to do

She held him until the police arrived, they told him he
Was lucky to be alive

All she had to say to the man as she walked away was
*"Get your head right, leave drugs alone, 'cuz when
You f**k with a Bull you'll get the horns!"*

Motion

I loved the way he pulled me into his arms and our bodies
Melded together in motion, we were hot like a five
Alarm fire, I immediately felt his desire

Strong arms wrapped around me in bed, he kissed
Me from my toes to my head, all the while speaking
Softly in my ear

Sexy is what he brought, I never thought I'd get sizzle like this
This man brought loving me to another level
Baby I am in heaven

His motion rocked its way between my thighs, opened my eyes
To things I never knew and spread eagle was the
Absolute best view

He moved deep, then deeper and touched my low and
High spots, I couldn't recover from being hot
He took me from the back when I touched my toes

I reached my climax over and over again
I never had this many with other men

It's all in his motions all in his strokes, his drive, his
Velvet touch and the extra long thrusts

Sticky with the smells of hot sweaty sex, I couldn't
Wait for him to show me, do me, use me, and fool me
I whispered Baby I'm ready for all your sex ....

What's next?

Nine to Five

She was working late and suddenly the office hottie was
Standing in the door, her breath caught in her chest and
She couldn't speak anymore

He stepped to her and she lost her hook-up
There was never a man she wanted so much

Before she knew it, his hand was up her skirt
He didn't seem surprised when he discovered
She wasn't wearing very much

They sprawled out on the desk and she spread her legs
He whispered in her ear he'd been thinking
About her for days

The sex was intense, he licked her face, put his
Tongue in her ear, leaned her over the desk and
Took her best

The next day, he didn't look her way. She called
Him and called him and he just ignored her
All day

He sent her a text and told her to stop riding his jock
Embarrassed and mad as hell, she was ready
To catch a case and go to jail

But, she had a better idea. You see the camera on her
Computer was on the whole time, a few clever edits and
Key strokes quickly had his naked ass online

He's definitely going to wish he had made the time

Ninth Degree

Ooooooooohhhhhh, Ooooooooohhhh, Ohhh, please, please
Get it! Get it! Right there, right there, get it!

Yessssss! Yessssss! That's it, here it comes, don't stop!
Hmmmmm, Yes, Baby!

I love it when you're on top! I just want it all the time
It's so damn good I don't want you to stop and I know
You will continue to blow my mind

Now lay with me, hold me, rub me, hmmm, that feels soooo good, your
Touch makes me shiver and tingle. I feel you rise on my backside
The next thing I know you're already inside, letting my dampness
Help your strokes glide

You make love to me to the ninth degree and you always
Bring me to my knees and that's good; I break our rhythm

Get off my back and bob my head; because I love using
The ball in my tongue I've seen how it makes
You feel.........

I love to see you writhing all over the bed
I love to hear you moan in deep, deep baritone

One stroke, two strokes and you are just about through
But, you'll stretch it out knowing you

I am here to please you like you please me, and I know
I have done that, when you help me up from my knees

No Guarantees

Her children ignore her and shout hateful words, she wonders
Is this what she gave her life for?

Her food comes with a side of sass; a dry sandwich with
Nothing more, it's not enough, they feed her like
She's on a fast

They complain when she needs something done
She's getting on their nerves, they don't have time
They got' a run

But, when her check comes in, they're right there
Nothing is left for her pleasure, what's left after bills
Buys them new high heels

She wants to enjoy what's left of her life. She was a good
Mother and a good wife, she took care of her family
Like she should, the good ones have gone to glory
If they were still here, this would not be her story

Disrespectful, hateful, spiteful, ungrateful, with no love
It's a sad situation that she'll never understand, because
The life she has is certainly not living

Why, oh why, can't they love her like she loved them?
They don't want to take care of her, like she took care of them
Their disrespect is killing her word by hateful word

There are no guarantees with the children you raise, you can
Only pray with all your might and pray for the best; that
They grow up and show you some respect

No More

After the break up her self-confidence was shattered
Getting with another man really didn't matter

She kept to herself, unsure of where her life was going
Her friends encouraged her to break out of her shell
It wasn't going to be easy she had gone through hell

Her tale is one that will warn others that abuse comes
In many forms, it's not just physical, black and blue
Eyes that a woman has worn

Mental, emotional and verbal abuse are not always seen
But the end results on a woman are pretty mean

A friend's intervention helped her realize that she was
Beautiful inside and out in everyone's eyes

Unsteady with low self-esteem, she learned to stand-up for herself
Build a new dream and finally feel that she is and always
Has been a valuable human being

No more being belittled, **No more** slaps upside her head
No more being called out of her name, **No more** giving up control
No more cutting up her clothes and **No
more** bruises with a bloody nose

She doesn't need a man to define her; she is her own woman now
She's been put down, run down, beat down and trampled upon

She survived those hard knocks and bumps, she survived the lumps
She stood up and out of his shadow with her head held high and is
Living her own life with her own voice

She is a survivor, a woman with goals and a story to be told

Not Now

He worked hard all day and when he got home what he
Wanted most was a cold beer and a good hot lay

She dealt with the kids, PTA meetings, cooking his food
Housework and so much more and none of these
Things put her in a sexy mood

She's too tired to be bothered and told him *not now,* he feels
Rejected and doesn't have any empathy, he wants what he needs
She'd better take heed

She challenged him to switch places with her to see how he'd fair
When she got home, she kicked up her feet and swigged a cold beer
All she could hear was him cussing and pulling
Out his hair

She stroked him and pulled at his pants, he smacked her hand
Away and told her *not now,* all he wanted to know
"Is how in the world do you do what you do?"

That day he gave her mad props for he was not aware how
Hard it was to do all that a wife does, so he relaxed his
Mean comments and harsh stare

With a new understanding they headed to bed, juices
Were flowing, legs were spread, toes were curling and
Not now never enter their heads

Not What He Seems

A good looking man that has everything on the ball
A good job, money in the bank, drives nice cars
Has his own home and stays away from
Neighborhood bars

He walks through the halls with his head held high and
Nods at the ladies as he passes by, all eyes are on
The bulge in his pants

Not one of us has been in bed with him, I made myself
A promise I would out do these women, I would be
The first to bed him down

True to my promise I wooed him and he couldn't resist
I am a brick house and there was no doubt he would not
Succumb to my feminine wiles

I was anxious to get him to bed, I wanted to show him
How good I am at giving head; but he seemed hesitant
And would not commit beyond dinner and drinks

So, I poured on more of my charms and he came to my
Place, he fidgeted and couldn't look me in the face

What's wrong with him I thought to myself, I tried to
Touch him and he pulled away

No matter, I was determined to have my way
I wanted him and I wanted to play

I threw myself on him and reached for his zipper
I was appalled and shocked to find out that
He was hiding a sock in his crotch

At work the next day, he didn't come my way
It's just as well, because by now every woman
In the building knew there was nothing to
That bulging swell

Out of the Box

His eyes rolled back in his head and his body quivered
And shook like an earthquake waking up the ground

He needs another round of that feeling tonight
She never says no, quiet as a mouse, he had
To have her in his house

She does whatever he wants. He turns to her
Strokes her hair and puts her to work

He loves her and she has what he needs in all the
Right places, she never complains and his end
Results are always the same

She never lets her man down, he never worries about
Her being out of place and she never nags him
About not giving her a taste

She's been meeting his needs every night and
He adores the only girl in his world

When he saw her for the very first time, he was excited
Right down to his dirty stinking black wool socks

He couldn't wait to get her home so he could blow her up
The minute he took her out of the box!

On the Bench

I couldn't get his attention away from the TV
I was horny and wanted him to play with me

He talks on the phone with his Buddies about
Football, Basketball or whatever, he covers it all

I love my man but this is not the way I want him
To spend all of his time

What about me, I have some needs that deserve
His attention

He eats, sleeps and talks about sports all the time
I've been naked in front of the TV screen and he
Shouted at me to move aside

Enough is enough; I am going to get tough
His nights out with the boys are about to get cut
Five nights out of seven is just too much

He listens to sports in the car on the radio
Oh hell no, this sh**t has got to go
We can't even have a conversation without
An interruption to check on scores

I left him with his sports addiction, because he
Didn't want to budge an inch and make some
Much needed time for his woman that he
Sidelined on the bench

Paradise

They lay on the pristine white sand of a Jamaican beach
While the beautiful crystal clear turquoise waters lapped over
Their glistening bodies and feet

He kissed her with urgency and rubbed her with hands that
Made her body melt

She loved everything about this tall gorgeous man, more than he could ever know
Their love for each other is something they never hesitated to show

Birds of paradise peeked out from rich green foliage and
Swayed in the soft warm ocean breeze

They were in an exotic land and they never lost sight, that
Under every palm tree there was a place they wanted to be
Sunning and washing themselves in the beautiful blue sea

Sweat drenched their naked bodies as they lay in each others arms
Under the Caribbean sun; a waterfall sent sprays of water to
Cool their writhing bodies, yet the heat between them prevailed

He rolled on top of her and left her with no doubt that he
Would love her well into the clear star filled skies of the night
Moving like a serpent she embraced his long strokes

She ran her hands up and down his back, she was ready for
His deep thrusts and another attack that made her body
Quiver and spout everything she had inside

She took him to the climax he'd been waiting for and
He did the same, for he loved it when she screamed
His name

Birds flew overhead singing love songs to them and as they lay
In each others arms, they realized that their love for each other
Is and always will be their ultimate paradise

Pay Day

He is successful and on the rise, he knows what he
Wants and he's keeping his eyes on the prize

He's living large, driving big cars, wearing the best
Clothes and making plenty of coin

Women are coming at him from all directions and
He can have his pick of the litter for the asking

In spite of his convictions to stay on track until he meets
A wife, a girl comes along and rocks his world, but
He knows for a fact she's *not* the one

She's been around the block and sees signs of the game he's
Playing but she has tricks of her own, so she plays along and
Lets him treat her like a one night stand

They drifted apart; months go by and he finds the woman
That he wants to give a wedding ring to along with his heart

The one night stand shows up once more, with her big belly crowding
The door and yells at him *"**Your** baby is on
The way, if you don't believe me
Check the DNA"*

He is stunned! He used a condom. How in the world is he
Going to tell his girl? This is one hell of a conundrum

The turkey baster method worked very well. She's looking
Forward to his big checks; if he doesn't pay up she'll
Be happy to ruin his good name and land his ass in jail

She's going to ride eighteen years on his gravy train
Not a bad pay day for a one night stand

Peace Out!

I heard you on the telephone when you didn't
Know I was home, bragging to your friend that
You always had me as your *go to bitch*
No matter what trouble you get in

I am tired, real tired and you need to know
That bailing your ass out of jail is not my lot
In life, I'm not your mother or your wife

I won't continue to be your *go to bitch* every
Time your dumb ass lands in a pinch

Try getting a job instead of chasing some
THOT out there to slob your knob

I'm not here to raise you. That was your momma's
Job and I'm not taking the fall because you
Turned out no good

Please believe me when I tell you, your mistakes
Are your own and you will not cuss me and
Disrespect me in my home

I mean it! Your *go to bitch* is moving on and
You better find yourself another home
Because you have ripped your ass with me

You better stay out of jail, or you'll be spending a lot of
Time with some guy named Bubba with the lights out
In a crowded cell

Your *go to bitch* is definitely saying
Good-bye, peace out and go to hell!

Reclamation

She had no man, twenty-five years ago he stepped
Out of her life and she felt rejected for years to come

She told herself she was alone but she wasn't lonely
Her battery operated toys were doing the trick
She didn't need a man, they were too slick

Then one day she had a service call and a dark chocolate
Man showed up at the door; he was bald and stood
Six-feet tall

He told her everything she needed to know about him but
Her self-esteem was so low; she could not believe he didn't
Have some trick up his sleeve

He called her and they made a date, after dinner
She invited him in even though it was late

The heat between them began to rise. When he undressed
She couldn't believe her eyes. Before she could react he
Quickly fell to his knees and spread her thighs

She thought her head would explode; more than ready to unload
She grabbed him, sucked him, rode him, he rode her and
She wouldn't let him stop

He put a hump in his back and he worked each and every crack
The coochie was tight and he worked hard to clean out twenty-five
Years of dust, to get deep into her pent-up lust

His bone was sore and he was weak in the knees, but he
Was more than ready and he aimed to please

He ravaged her over and over again and
She begged him not to stop
She could feel him go deeper when she was on top

No problem, he drove his sore bone deep and hard, he had
Something to prove, he wanted her and he was happy to help
Her reclaim her groove

Say What?

"Here I stand hot and ready to rock your world but
You didn't have one kind word to say, to your girl

"Talk about killing the mood, I wanted to caress
You and uplift you - that's what I do
But, lately it seems it's not enough for you"

"Kill the mood, attitude, now what's a girl to do?
Whatever it is you're going through, I hope
You work it out, because I am too sexy
To be without"

"Say what?" You heard me. I said "I am too sexy
To be without, so, if you continue to pout
Know this, you can count me out!"

"Because as sure as I'm standing here, there is
Another man out there that would love for
Me to put my tongue in his ear"

"Leave hot kisses on his neck and drive his
Body to tremble as I run my hand up and
Down his shaft and you know how good
I am at my craft"

"So, lose the attitude I have desires that need to be met
Get over here put your fingers inside me and make
Me wet then bring me to a climax I
Won't forget"

"Next time, I'm naked at the door don't even speak
Take off your clothes so we can get on our freak
Because I am too sexy to go without
That meat"

"Say what?" "You heard me!"

Shattered Peace

Sitting in a quiet room, contemplating the sights and
Sounds that surround your quiet mind, you wonder
How long it will last before your peace is shattered and
Pushed aside

Outside, the mowers and blowers are going, the traffic is flowing
Children chase the music that sucks, coming out of
The ice cream truck

Gunshots, ring out in the night, making people stop drop and roll
The gun violence is way out of control. Sirens scream
Through the town and you think that peacefulness
Will never be found

Loud voices, televisions blaring, dogs barking
Kids laughing with music bumping, brings you
To the reality, that your quiet mind, will shut out
The noise and focus on the peacefulness

You close your eyes and push out the light, to see images
On the dark side of your lids and you are taken to places of
Peacefulness away from where you live

She Wanted More

He loved his woman with all his heart, they moved in
Together after he bought her a house

Sixty-hour work-weeks, paying all the bills, he gave his
Girl everything in the world

But it never seemed to be enough, she always wanted more
Seems like every time she came through the door she had
New items that he didn't buy and he began to suspect that
There was another guy

She wanted more alright; she humped her boyfriend and
His so called friend night after night

With flowers and candy in hand he came home early to
The surprise of his life

His homeboy took advantage of his girl being alone and
They disrespected him in his home

Harsh words were spoken, a friendship was broken, tempers flared
A fight broke out and when it was over, her actions had left no doubt
That he would never turn this Ho into a housewife

Shiny Red Boots

She slides on red patent leather thigh high boots, with six-inch heels
A red leather corset accentuates her tiny waist and breast
She's expecting a guest

Everything is ready for him; there he is at the door
She leads him in by his tie to a room in the back

The room is covered in red velvet and bathed in candlelight
He undresses and she commands him to sit naked on the floor
He immediately sits up to beg, he's done this many times before

She commanded him to lick her boots "Yes Mistress"
He does as he is told she's been doing this routine with him
Since she was nineteen years old

Clamping his nipples and twisting hard, daring him
To scream, she commanded him to say nothing
He obeys; she is his dream

Whipping, whipping and more whipping; the tip of the
Whip comes down hard across his body
This is how he gets his pleasure for him this is ecstasy

"Now, crawl dog and bark. "Lie on your back and spread your legs"
"Yes Mistress"

She attaches shackles to his wrists and ankles, stretching him
Until it hurts, but he won't tell her to stop, for this is
What he needs to quench his sexual thirst

From his very first time, he thought this was a hoot
Now, as he loses consciousness the last thing he
Sees are those shiny red patent leather boots

Shout Out!

Shout out!

To Detroit where I was born and raised
The Inland Empire is where I live these days

Riverside, Corona, Chino, Fontana, Rialto and Ontario
These are the diverse communities that
Make our neighborhoods flow

Shout out!

To all the Homies that come to the basement to
Showcase their special talents and have
A good time

The host is a master of the mike. He hypes the
Crowd and prepares them for the night
It's open mike for those with the nerve to try

Poetry, comedy and good music too, gives
The audience a peek at who's new

Favorites grace the stage to make you
Laugh, sway to the music, sweat and want
To go home and do the do

Shout out!

To the Inland Empire
It's where we live, it's where
We thrive, it's where we
We groove and come alive!

Signifying Monkey

The clique loves to talk smack behind your back
Making all kinds of wise cracks

The loud mouth signifies the most, keeping the
S**t going and spilling the tea

She never comes right out and says what's
Really going on, she talks loud, huffs and puffs
Throwing venom on others as she struts her stuff

She is the boss of her little playmates
They're too afraid to speak out against her for
Fear she will make them the next target
So, they step back and don't argue

She's just like the monkey in the jungle swinging
From tree to tree telling everybody's business
Spewing out hurtful things, so she can
Try and stay relevant on the popular scene

Then one day, the signifying monkey met
Her match, a boss chick stepped on to the scene
With fire in her eyes, she took out the signifying
Monkey and made her a laughing stock

Suddenly, the signifying monkey had no more gossip
No more tea, she kicked rocks so hard she
Flew across the jungle and slammed into a tree

The boss chick had this message for signifying monkey's everywhere
"Bullies you better watch out because you never know
When your cowardly ass will run up on someone like me!"

Simone

Simone lays awake waiting for him to come home
He's out sowing his oats she knows he's not alone

Taking care of the children, working two jobs she
Wonders what she can do to make him come home

Simone grows tired of waiting for him and her courage
Starts to rise, just yesterday he blackened both of her eyes

No more beatings for her, no more lonely nights
She's going to take her children and take flight

He looks all over town and finally tracks her down
He threatens her and calls her names; he starts
Toward her with his fists balled up

She screams and turns to run, but he's quick to pull
Out his gun, he doesn't hit her, he shoots their son

The police are too late, they haul him away
He'll rot in jail forever and a day

Simone, grieves the son she had and moves forward
With her other children without their dad

Now that she's free, she can be anything
She wants to be, he won't be holding her back
She can finally get a life and get on the right track

Skills

The house is dark when he arrives and unlocks
The door, no one is home. He loosens his tie
And wipes the tiredness from his eyes

He fixes a Martini and sits alone in the living room
Looking through the window at a view of the ocean
Under the silvery moon

Suddenly, he hears a soft sound and looks around
Nothing is there anywhere

He hears the sound again and walks through the house
The soft sound gets closer he becomes quiet as a mouse

He eases open the bedroom door and there she is naked
Covered only by the light of the moon. Her eyes are closed
Her legs are spread and she looks beautiful lying on the bed

She caresses her ample breasts and squeezes the nipples
Raising her head to lick and flick, she slides her
Hands down her body she knows plenty of tricks

Reaching the "V" between her legs, she begins to stroke
He's holding himself back, about to choke on a gasp as
She puts her fingers deep inside and never opens her eyes

Her head tosses side to side as her fingers continued to glide
He watched from the door and his manhood began to rise through
The fly of his pants and he wanted to see more

While thrashing about, gyrating and pulsating, she called his
Name as she released her treasure without shame

He stroked himself, he was ready to unload. She opened
Her eyes and realized what he had seen. She ran to him
Dropped to her knees, without gagging or spitting
And skillfully finished his stream

Skin

His skin touches my skin I feel the weight
Of his body on mine as he rises and falls
While our bodies are intertwined

Friction brings the heat, heat brings the
Sparks, water beads, we both have needs

Ahhhhhh, s**t! The spell is broken when the skin
Gets in the way from baby to man it was never
Cut away

Hurry! Pull it back, hold it back and get in there and
Prepare to attack, save the moment, float my boat
The lust inside me is bubbling up and up and up.....

Ohhhhh yeaah, that's it! Right there, you're so good
My eyes roll back in my head and I finally erupt!

No thanks to that skin you almost didn't get it in
Remove that hood and let the real fun begin!

Sleeping With the Enemy

He loved her day and night, night and day
He loved her in every way

She didn't get out of bed for three whole days
The loving was so good she couldn't count
The ways

He kissed her feet, he licked her toes beneath the sheets and
Worked the little man with his tongue until he fell out of the boat
Her body trembled all over as her climax peaked
She felt the cramp in her legs relax as they
Both released

Over and over she felt his might, he worked her so
Hard her kitty was swollen like it had been in a fight
He worked that pink pussy like never before

When she finally came up for some air; days had passed
She finally combed her hair and got off her ass

She couldn't shake the feeling that something wasn't right
Her girlfriend called and confirmed her fears. Her new
Man is the leader of the gang that robbed her house
She was sleeping with the enemy

Her heart was broken and she was pissed off, he played
Her and that wasn't cool, she had slept her way to
The bottom; but vowed he would not laugh at her
Like she was some fool

She slept with the enemy and now that was done
He was going to feel her wrath from the barrel
Of her big gun

Or maybe not, she knew how to teach him a lesson
She invited her male friends to run a train on him and
They did, over and over and over again

These days he's on a street corner selling his ass
Big Bertha is big time pimping and she don't play when it
Comes to her cash

Smack Down!

He rolls to his side of the bed and pulls
The covers over his head

She wonders what's going on, for weeks
There's been no hot love making
In their home

He has a headache, or a leg cramp, he tells
Her to stop nagging and leave him alone

A plan began to form in her head
Something smelled fishy, so she
Called on her girl, Bloody Redd

They found him with his woman
Strolling through the mall

The smack down was quick
She gave him three chops to the
Throat and put him down with a swift
Hard kick to the d**k

She tore that ass down to the white meat and
Out of the frame; she couldn't stop calling
Him out of his name

Now, he **really** won't be smashing
For a whole lot of nights

She stepped over him and let him know
His clothes would be on the lawn and
She didn't care if he had no where to go

Let this be a lesson to cheater's everywhere
What's done in the darkness will eventually come
To the light, so get your big and little heads
Together and treat your woman right

Smooth Manipulator

When he saw her long shapely legs, round tight butt, flat belly
And little waist, he vowed to his crew, she'd be his
In a matter of days

He knew he was in love; he put on his best rap, his game was
Tight like hand and glove

She succumbs to his charm and becomes the woman that graces
His arm, he is generous and attentive. She is happy as can be

She wants to hang out with her girls, they've always
Been apart of her world

He sees things differently; he wants her home with him
He doesn't want her to go out with them, work out at
The gym, or wear the short skirts that pulled him in

He tells her she's gained weight, it's not safe for her
To be out late, he says her girls don't have a man
They just want to talk about him and hate

The way she was isn't good enough anymore, he was
Manipulating her into changing her life

She can't believe what she's hearing; but wants to please him
So she changes her ways and spends most of her days alone
Now, he can't find time to be home

He's in the streets, hanging at the club. A phone call from
Her girls woke her from the nightmare she's been in
She packed her s**t and hit the road, she woke up and
Broke his control

Sounds in the Night

The sunset closes out the day and makes way for
The darkness of night, a time to rest and renew
Breathe deep and prepare for sleep

Suddenly I am awakened; I shake my head to clear my
Groggy thoughts and listen to the muffled sounds coming
Through the walls

I strain to hear what the voices are saying and a woman
Screams in ecstasy from the depths of her throat
The bed springs are squeaking and squealing frantically from
What she's hollering he is tearing up the little man
In the boat

The noise of sex is in the air and they are
Getting their groove on without a care

Car horns blare, winos argue in the alley below and
Sirens whine as they rush by the Black Madonna's Shrine
On Linwood and Chicago

No sleep for me, I boil a cup of tea and look out at
What there is to see, traffic lights, women walking the streets
Low riders with music bumping and hydraulics jumping

The couple upstairs in apartment 203 is still squeaking
Squealing and hollering so loud, I can't even hear my TV
He is doing the damn thang and I'm just curious to
Know his name

No, there won't be any sleep for me. I am enjoying
The sounds in the darkness of the night and all the things
It brings to life

Swirl

She's built like a wide track Pontiac and has a
Body by Fisher, she knows how to make it talk
When she walks, it's enough to give me a heart attack

We met in the lunch room at work and began to talk
During dinner I am surprised to see that she has
The look of lust in her eyes

She confesses to me, that she noticed me too
She just didn't want to make the first move

We stopped off for drinks and continued our fun
Dancing, kissing and rubbing each other on the arm

The night passes quickly and I take her home, I went in
For a nightcap, she grabbed me and it was on

I caressed her small perky breasts, they were just right
Anything over a mouthful is a waste. I kissed her neck
Her thighs and sucked in between, her body is defined
And very lean

She led me to her bedroom and threw me on the bed
Before I knew it she began suckling me like she was
Looking for milk, then dropped down between
My legs

I love making love to and being loved by soft pink pussy
When we rub them together the friction ignites my body
Into the stratosphere

Real d**k, no way, get the hell out' a here
Go somewhere and have another beer

I know how to love her body and she knows mine
We definitely do what's needed without the swine

Girl on girl is the only way we swirl!

Switch Up

Red, red lips short skirts and the highest of heels
Gives a man all kinds of thrills

You're classy, yet sexy without showing much skin
This is what makes him want to touch you over and
Over again

Keep yourself together, because the same kind of
Look you had when you first met, is what keeps
You on his mind

He will insist you change your style over time
But, don't let him take you off your grind

Jealousy can make a man crazy, thinking every man
Is looking at you, he'll want to hide you away and
Keep you from going out to play

He knows long grandma skirts, old T-shirts and
Sweats do not make a man want to flirt

So heed my words pretty girls, the same thing you
Used to lure him may be come a double edged sword

The Beginning

Tonight he would celebrate his twenty-first birthday and
Hang out with his boys, drinking and fist
Bumping and bringing the noise

The strip club was jumping, his heartbeat was pumping
The girl straddling his lap was off the hook
He loved the way she looked

He wound up in the hotel with her. He was excited to
Be there and you could definitely tell by the
Swell in his pants

She undressed him with her eyes and slowly pulled off
His pants revealing his size, he wanted what she was
Offering especially after she started to dance

She climbed on top easing him inside and
With her wetness it was an easy slide

Pop, pop, pop, the kitty, stop and lock
Then slowly......
Rock, rock, rock the hips from side to side
Her double clutch took his breath away and
Brought more heat between his thighs

She moved slowly up and down like she was
Riding a Merry-Go-Round, she rode his pole
Deeper and deeper into the rabbit hole

Her body movements were off the chain
Off the glass, off his tip, she made him holl'a
His climax was so intense he bit through his lip!

Yes, his introduction to twenty-one was over and done
Losing his virginity; however was just the beginning
Of a lot more of these nights to come

The Bottle

He had a good life, two kids, a beautiful wife
And a career as an Engineer

One by one, loved ones passed on and he was left alone
The bottle becomes his friend; inside it he thinks
He sees the end

But, by the grace of God he is pulled from the deep dark
Abyss, by loving hands that brought him back to
Holding his head up high and knowing once
Again what it is like to be a man on the rise

His son loves his father enough to keep him close
And repays him for the love and dedication he
Gave him over his lifetime without remorse

The bottle is no longer an issue, he is living his life
The way he should, he's with loved ones now and
That makes him feel very good

He is forever grateful to the son that took him in and
Saved him from giving the devil his soul and
Living a life of loneliness, despair and sin

The Collector

He loved women, all women, it didn't matter to him
If they went to the gym, had a limp and wasn't slim

He was all about what he could get from them
That's all that mattered to him

What he wanted was what he needed at the time
He would scratch out every dime from each and
Every one of them

He was the collector of what they had; he made it his
Business to extract their goods, right down to their
Pink panties, black panties, red panties, hell no panties

Money, cars, a big cabin in the woods, he wore
The best clothes with jewelry fit for a king

Until one day......

He stepped to a bad ass chick that took him
Down in the ring, she was slicker than he
Was and she was good

Before he knew it, she had boosted his cabin in the
Woods, he was dazed and amazed at how swift she
Was and how she was able to snatch all of his
Worldly goods

How the hell did he let that happen?
He got twisted in her panties

Game recognized game
There is no honor among thieves so she happily took him
To his knees and walked away with his draws
Because elite hustlers like her live by street laws

The Reward

In the neighborhood where he lives the street lights are out
What's lurking in the darkness could cost you your life
Even for him it is a fright

He's just out to get some milk from the store
His mother works hard and he likes helping
Her with the chores

They don't have much money and he does what
He can, he's been the main man since he was eight
He tried to take his father's place

The hair stands up on the back of his neck
On his way back home, something tells
Him that he is not alone

From the shadows between the buildings the
Hoodies emerge, the bullets ran through
Him like an electrical surge

The Hoodies disguised their angry eyes and
They looked down on him and what they saw
Was a clean cut young man that they despised

The Hoodies ran from the scene as their laughter rang
Through his ears. Living in the hood and catching
A bullet were his mother's worst fears

The Hoodies didn't get away and the young man
Lived to tell his story another day. He was a
Straight A honor student with life to celebrate

He continued his journey in life and went on
To know much success

His greatest reward was going back to the place where
He almost lost his life; so he could do some good and
Teach other young men they too could get
Out of the hood

The Ride

He's been out all night with his boys, it's
Five O'clock in the morning and my
Jaws are tight

When he comes back I'll hold my ground, I'll
Beat him down with my frowns, harsh words
And anything else I can think of......

Here he comes with that stupid grin on his face
Rubbing all over me; he melts me like butter and
Makes my heart flutter

He knows just what to do –
He laid me down, melted my frown and
Kissed away my harsh words

He makes me so hot my body sizzles from the
Heat we generate between the sheets

He flipped me on top maintaining fierce, piercing eye contact
He said dirty, nasty, filthy things to me. I couldn't stop
Pumping up and down, faster and faster and faster
I wanted everything inside to come down

I rolled over on my back and he rode me hard like a
Racehorse on the track and put me away real wet

It's episodes of lovemaking like this I'll never forget
If this is my reward after his night out with his boys

I'll play along, so I can take this ride every time
He comes home

Three Hearts

His boys looked up to him; how in the world did he
Control two women in his life? One of them
His woman the other one his wife

He loved both of them and couldn't live without either one
He took his woman to live with him and wifey
So they could make a home

He worked real hard to make ends meet, while his women
Went shopping, made love to each other and ran the streets
They were never home and he began to suspect that
Something was wrong

He hired detectives to hang around and watch their every
Move and what he found set him off and put him in
A foul mood

The video was very clear, they both met with a man
In the park, had sex in his car and drank beer

When he found out he went crazy and saw red; that's
When he lost it and shot them all in the head

Three hearts no longer beat as one
Why did they have to cheat and mess with his damn fun?
Those days are over – the justice system had no problem
Putting a needle in his arm

His boys lowered their heads, with the lesson learned
One woman was plenty for their beds

Tough Love

I love you to death and I have gone through the fire for you
There is always something you need me to do and
There is nothing I wouldn't do

Just know and please remember, I will not stand for your
Disrespect cussing me out and calling me names
The first time you raised your hand to me I saw flames

If you ever try and put your hands on me, I promise you this
I won't hesitate to put a cap in your ass, there are some things
I just will not let pass

You borrow my car, take money from my purse and I can't
Get you to bring me a dinner, my hair is getting thinner and
I'm not getting any rest because of all your mess

I will finish what I started. I brought your ass in this
World and I will take your ass out!

I want you to understand that my tough love is
Strong love, tenderness and stepping away

I will let you go and hope you come to know one day
That tough love is and was the only way

I'll let you take a guess at how this chapter will end
It's time for your ass to step off and get out of my face

Now, you'll really have something to pout about
I've already packed your s**t, it's time for you to get out!

Trail of Tears

Many attended the celebration of the season
A happy occasion that ended in a tragic
Way for no reason

Cowards reared their ugly heads and
Rounds of bullets went everywhere

Fourteen lay dead while others nursed their
Wounds and realized their worst fears
When it was over there was a trail of tears

We will overcome this tragic event, we
Will *not* be bullied in our homeland
In this Inland Empire, we *will*
Take a stand!

We will never forget that day in San Bernardino
We will *never* forget loved ones lost
We will continue in their memory
To live our lives at any cost

Shoulder to shoulder we will look forward to a
Brighter day and we will be victorious in our quest
To find a way to bring peace to all this unrest

We are the Inland Empire and we are strong!
We live on to show our strength, we will walk down
Our trail of tears, until we can calm our fears ....
Just know, it may take many years

Troubles

You try to keep appearances on the outside - happy and upbeat
You don't want your face to tell your troubles to anyone walking
Down the street

You hold on to troubles that grind inside your
Gut wearing out your body and mind

Inside your head your mind never rests, you think
Is this just another test?

Another test, to set you up for what's down the line, something
That is and will be better than what's happening at this time

Roiling on the inside but staying cheerful on the outside
Helps bring positive energy to chase away the blues and
Keep the outside and inside from being fused

Hiding your troubles behind the mask on your face
Frees them from your gut and the sour taste that destroys
Your positive thoughts; staying positive helps the
Inside from being distraught

Try not to worry about what happened last or what may happen
Tomorrow, live for today in the moment and let your
Troubles melt away

Two Kinds of Love

Let me love you the way I know how
I promise, I will use all my experience
To make you say wow

I'll begin with just the right kiss that's not too wet
To start a slow burn inside; so baby relax
Close your eyes; because I am definitely going to
Increase your size

Another kiss more urgent this time, now I can feel
You really unwind I know what makes you tick

I'm going to lick, lick, lick, like it's a Popsicle on a stick
I know you'll love my butterfly flick; top to bottom
Nothing will be missed, I aim to please and
Give you pure bliss

I know when to tighten it, slow it down, stop it or
Move it around, your climax will be off the hook
See, here it comes! I know that look, keep it coming
I'm prepared to do more

Pull my hair, smack my ass, all that does is make
Me *better* at my task, I control the flow, I can
Make it fast or slow and *that* will drive you wild

You better *know* you are not playing
With a child

When you're inside me I won't flinch, there is
Nothing you can do to make me wince. I know
All the tricks from both sides of the fence

How you ask did I get all of my experience?

I'm a pretty woman that use to have a d**k!

Up the Wall

He watched her lounging and recalled how she moved
Her body as he backed her up against the wall

She cried out for him to go slow and easy, he knew he
Was hung from stem to stern, he'd sent many women
To the emergency room to see an intern

He was very well endowed, yes indeed, she would
Take every inch and he would succeed in giving
Her the best sex she'd ever had, but backing up
The wall and running from him made him mad

They smashed through her moans of agony and finally
When her sweaty body went limp with exhaustion
He released her from his hold; because sexing her
Never gets old and no matter what she says
He'll hit that any day and every way he can
He wants to show her and he wants her to
Remember that he will be her only man

She was thinking, I can't take this, day in and day
Out he never gives my kitty a break; I just want
To run and hide, I don't care about my pride what
I do care about, is what he's doing to my insides

He isn't gentle or kind and he doesn't take his time
He thinks being well endowed is all it takes and
That kind of thinking is a real big mistake

Running from his thrust was all she could do to
Save herself for someone new, she left him a note
So her words wouldn't get caught in her throat

She wrote... A huge d**k doesn't always do the trick

Where Have I Gone?

Where have I gone? I look in the mirror and I don't see
The me I remember me to be

I have given so much of me to so many others that I
Don't have enough left for myself

My motivation has evaporated into thin air and now
I look at the things I loved to do and I just don't care
So every day, I just sit in my favorite chair

I've hit a wall of depression and I can't recall how
It used to be, before I gained weight while eating
In front of the TV

I'm lost and I'm looking for myself, the one I had to
Put aside to take care of someone else

Where have I gone? When do I do me? I need to
Find myself to recover the things I've lost:

My self-motivation, self-preservation, a slamming body
The attitude of a bad ass hottie and the joy I once had

I don't have any regrets on doing what needed to be done
I will forever remember and appreciate all the time
I had with my loved ones

I gave them my strength, my power, my energy, I gave them my all
Yes, I sacrificed and I wouldn't hesitate to do it over again, knowing
My heart will be broken leaving me shattered
Worn and forlorn in the end

I need to be selfish now and go deep inside my body and mind
To dust myself off, pick myself up and move on
So I will recap:

With what I've learned, I *will* be a better me, I *will* find myself
Love myself and return to being all I *know* I can be
I *will* regain my self-motivation, self-appreciation, and self-worth
Re-claim my turf and make sure, that my presence is
Known on this earth

Where You At?

"Hola Papi! Hurry home tonight, 'cause
When you get here, I'll be ready for you lying
On my back"

"I'm muy caliente and as usual I won't disappoint you
I'll be dressed in my nurse's uniform, waiting for
You with a big fat joint"

"Candlelight, soft music and a hot bubble bath
I'll get wet as you kiss my slippery tight ass
Let's take our time I want this night to last"

"When you rise and erupt, I won't choke
I'll drink it down like it's a sugar-free coke
So mi corazon, don't be late, I want you and
I don't want to wait."

Hours later she calls again

"Hola Papi! Where you at? The bath is cold, dinner
Is old and I'm tired of lying on my back!"

"I'm not waiting another minute, I'm pissed and there is
Nothing I want from you. The night is ruined
Where the hell are you?"

She put on her clothes and headed for the door
She vowed she didn't what his ass anymore

Then lo and behold, she sees him in the club
With his arm around a friend of hers

Drinks are thrown, weaves are blown and
She blacked his eye as she left for home

What a night; certainly not what she planned
But she knows him and he'll come around tomorrow
With his d**k in his hand, because he has big cojones and
She likes that about her man

While He's Away

While he's away I must continue my day, work a
Job so I can get paid, tend to the children's needs
Little Angel, broke her arm, I still feel the sensation
Of alarm

While he's away, I write letters every day, send cookies
In a box along with my hair locks

While he's away, I miss him so very much, it's
All we can do to keep up our phone sex

My toys help ease the urges and I fight them every day
Because I promised him I would not stray

I love him very much and one day soon I'll feel
His touch

He finally comes home to me and is restless and
Rude, he's giving me big time attitude

I'm pissed off and tell him so, "*What about the
Love you had for me when you were away
What about those love letters you wrote
Professing your love day after day?*"

I've been naïve; he was just telling me what I wanted
To hear, it seems he doesn't remember the things
He said were dear

Now, all he wants to do is hang with his boys and
Spend all the money I bring home
I bring home. How quickly he forgets; it took all this time for me
To see him for whom he really is

I never thought he would treat me this way. But, he left me for
Someone else yesterday and he doesn't even look my way

That's okay! Because I won several million dollars in the
Lotto the very next day!

CYNTHOLOGY
A Collection of Rhymes

Book II – *Electrified*

READER FAVORITES

Always Near

August 07, 2012
(My mom's Sunset)

Today, I feel like going for a walk
So I can talk with you. I am quiet as I listen
To all the things you tell me I should do

Gone but never far away, I feel your presence
By me every day

A little bird comes to my yard, sits on
The fence and looks at me. I know
You're watching your messages are clear

Losing you was my greatest fear
I'm not worried now because I know
You may be gone from here but you
Are always near

Ashes

Ashes represent broken dreams, disappointments
Failures, hurts and lost loved ones

Mourning should be for a season and not a lifetime
Stop mourning over what you can not change
Forgive betrayal, let go of your questions and the blame

Stop living in the rearview mirror of life
Look through the big windshield that shows you
The way to a future that is greater than your past

The enemy loves to see you sitting in the ashes
Feeling sorry for yourself, get up dust those ashes off
Hold your head up high and spit in the enemies' eye

One door closes and another one opens to show
You a bigger better future and a brighter day
Look to the future and **blow** those ashes away

Bad Kitty

Bad Kitty is on the prowl, night after night
She puts on her high heels, great big hair
Puffs her nose and leaves her lair

Bad Kitty, is full of revenge, she's had her
Fill of selfish, egotistical, abusive men
The only thing on her mind now, is getting even

The last man she had wasn't cool, he sexed her
And didn't use anything to protect his tool

For her it's too late, she was too naïve
She let him touch her without a rubber sleeve
Of course he never mentioned he had a disease

Now Bad Kitty is a hot mess; she's on fire
And not in a good way, she's out for
Revenge and someone is going to pay

She's in the club and finds a new love, they
Head for bed and sex their way to a sweaty frenzy
She was successful in getting him to keep it real
She told him she liked the way *bareback* feels

No raincoat, no hat, Bad Kitty passed on
The disease that made her hot, she knows
What she did was not right
But, she'll keep sharing night after night

She's full of revenge, so look out men
Bad Kitty is looking for you, avoid her tease
And please, use a sleeve when you feel the need
Or you'll go out like Bad Kitty with a fatal disease

Faking It

We met in the elevator and I caught him
Giving me the side eye. I spoke up and we
Made a date, I told him not to be late

After a great dinner and drinks we decided
To dash, bodies were heating up and
We went to his place to crash

His athletic build turned me on
Broad shoulders, tiny waist
Hugh thighs ripped and tight
I was looking forward to an
Exciting night

He did all the right things, he liked
Playing with my nipple ring
Neither one of us was shy and I
Thought, I picked the right guy

I was in for a shock when he
Pulled off his pants, his tool was
The size of my thumb and
Could barely be seen; this was
Turning out to be a bad dream

He didn't realize the rest of his manhood
Was sucked up inside that athletic build

He tried and tried; but he could not make me squeal
So I laid there and faked it so good, there was no
Way he'd know, his little man really wasn't a big deal

For Your Pleasure

I want to please you and do what you want me to do
Baby tell me how you want it and I will give it to you

Face down in the pillow, face to face, I want you to have
It in the right place, just the way you want it
Come on let's give it a go, I'm ready
To give you a nasty show

On the bed, on the table, in the corner
I have never been so damn horny. I'm here to please you
I'll do it all, c'mon let's do it up against the wall

Tell me what you want me to do, I have
Some new tricks for you, always willing to try
You are my girl and I am your guy

I love caressing your body tenderly
I love entering you gingerly and taking you
To the place you love to be and those sweet
Sounds you're making are all because of me

I'll give you what you want, where and when
You want it, any time you want it

It pleasures me to pleasure you, I'll always give you
My very best, I will make you happy or I will not rest

I'll take your climax off the chart and
When I feel you release and explode
Then and only then, will I release my load

129

Ghetto Candy

Her name is Candy and she lives in the hood
She's a product of what other people say is no good
Dad left a long time ago; Momma pays the rent being a Ho
Baby brother went to jail again for cutting his woman on the chin

Life is different here in the hood; but Candy lives like a queen
Strutting around in her skin tight jeans, ribbons of gold-red
Extensions showing in her hair, false nails in bright colors
That blinds the eye. She steps to the car with a bag of grass
She vowed to herself she would not be the one selling her ass

She's seen how people live on the other side of town
She's in this ghetto life right now and it is what it is
But she refuses to let it get her down. Surviving day in
And day out, one day at a time, when you live in
The ghetto that's all you ever have on your mind

She sells her stash and has plenty of cash to move to another level
She's going to move far away and beat the devil. She plans
To come back and pull someone else from this ghetto prison
So they too can experience a different kind of living

Like millions of other young teens Ghetto Candy is in the
Prime of her life with plenty of dreams; but she was cut down
In a hail of gunfire on her way to the other side of town
Now it's over for her as they lower her casket into the ground

Bullets flying young people dying for no reason at all
Black and Brown and that's not all who want to see the
Violence end, so there will be no more Ghetto Candy's
Losing out on their dreams

Honey I'm Home

I was naked at the door when he came home from work
I kissed him and began to unbutton his shirt
He started to protest; but I covered his mouth and throat
With kisses, he dropped his head back, closed his eyes
And moaned softly, as I stroked between his thighs

I don't want tame sex; I want a rough ride tonight
He put his hand on my ass and I whispered grab it
Grab my ass and hold it tight, spread it, rub it
Grind it and let me know you love it

Grab it and find my groove, move inside me
With your talented tool, back and forth
To and fro, rub it, grind it, hold it; pump it
Ride it, smack it and let your white lava flow
Bite my lip and whisper you love me
Then come back for more

Now, what was it you wanted to say when you
Walked through the door?

Karma

Karma is a bitch, is what people say
When people do you wrong, trust and believe
They will have their day

You may not be around to see it happen, but
Karma keeps track and knows when to strike
It never forgets, even though they might

When someone is mean and nasty, hateful and rude
Always walking around with an attitude
Spewing foul words at you out of their mouth

Just know they can't be happy and they'll
Have plenty to say, just step to the side and
Get out of their way

Karma is a bitch, oh yes, it is and anyone who
Thinks they can avoid it really hasn't lived

However you choose to live your life
Good or bad, Karma knows what to do
Sorrow or joy is what's in store for you

So think about your actions and keep
Karma in mind, because you better believe
You'll reap what you sow over time

Peep Show

I see you standing in your window and
You are staring back at me. I am startled by your
Nakedness and watch as you begin to play

I think to myself, this is exactly the way I like starting my day
You begin with slow moves to some unheard groove as
You toss your hair into the air

You caress your breast and I can only imagine how silky
Your skin is and I want to touch you very much

You turn your back and touch your toes; this is a move
I can tell that you know very well

From the back, I am mesmerized at the space between your thighs
I am numb, yet my body begins to respond to the sight and
I stand in the window well into the night

You fascinated me with all of your moves, especially the one –
Well you know, the one that hit me hard and I was done

Now, every time I pass my window I look your way, hoping to have
Another wonderful day; but this time with your invitation to
Come over and play

Pretty Eyes

The Pretty Eyes are all glammed up
Beautiful colors and jewels adorn what they see
They are wise and knowing and
Their first look of the day always, delves inside of me

Pretty Eyes in a beautiful face, what secrets do you disguise
Sadness, laughter, happiness and joy
The Pretty Eyes have seen these things before

Pretty Eyes smile through the years, along the journey of life
Shedding lots of tears, once wide eyed an innocent, saw
Innocence fade away

Pretty Eyes speak volumes without saying a word and can
Cut through a man without raising a hand

Years bring more knowledge that is kept inside, but
You can see that wisdom shine through the Pretty Eyes

Sex Addiction

She never blends in, she always stands out
Luscious full lips that she loves to pout
Beautiful almond shaped eyes, smoldering
Like red hot embers from deep down inside
She's on the prowl and there is no shame in her game
When it comes to her addiction, she has no pride

She exudes sex appeal that is relentless
Sensual feelings bubble up from her core
She thinks of sex all the time; nothing more
The vision of his body on hers takes control

She is addicted to her desire for sex, her body craves the
Constant rush and that is how the addiction came to be
She wants a well endowed man to quench her needs
She has to have the warmth of his mouth and seed

Addicted to sex, not love, she searches
For sex and not love; because love hurts
And sex never does, it's the pleasure
She craves, not someone to love

Licking, rubbing, groaning, penetrating
Arching her back to meet his thrust, then releasing
With wild screams of joy, she sighs as she reaches
To touch the wetness between her thighs. Her body quivers
As she regains control, it's at times like this she loses her soul

Oh yes, this is what she lives for every day, all day
Sultry as hell, she uses what she has
To get the men she needs day after day
She has one question.....

Do you want to play?

The Closet

I'm in the closet peeping out trying to see what gay life
Is all about, I'm still not sure if I want to come out

Mom and Dad won't be happy with me and
I know people will certainly judge me
Just because I want to be what deep down
Inside my soul tells me I should be

Should I come out, or not, should I come out, or not?
I really want to leave this closet life, I want to be
Myself in the broad daylight

The closet hides me and hears my confessions and it
Is where I keep my gay possessions

I want to come out, be out, shout out I'm gay and
I'm proud, I will, I'll come out – but maybe not
I don't know if I have the strength to deal

Time goes by and I realize, the closet imprisons me
I have grown and now I *know* that I will never be happy
If I don't live the life that is meant for me

I've left the closet and I am free! It no longer hides me
I am strong and confident, my head is held high
I'm out of the closet and I will be gay
Until the day I die!

What a Man Wants

I was sitting at the bar in the club when my attention
Was captured by a beautiful girl

Dressed in designer clothes, hair done with nice looking
Nails and toes, I decided this was a woman
I wanted to know

I offered her a drink and we enjoyed each others' company
She invited me to her home for the night
When I walked in what I saw gave me a fright

There were clothes, shoes and purses everywhere
Empty take out containers and lots of cat hair
This chick was nasty I just wanted to run

Her room and the bed was a mess
How in the hell could I even think about
Making love to her. I made excuses and
Told her I had to go

I was turned off and even as good as she looked
I was not about to land my hook; no way
Was I getting in bed with her; not knowing
If her hygiene was up to par, I got
In my car and went back to the bar

I needed a drink to think about what I saw
She came to the bar looking for a man that
Would look pass her mess; with one thing
On his mind and that's to get under her dress

So, ladies check this out and keep this in mind
Many men out here are just like me. We're looking
For the total package, not just a good time and a freebie

Why Did I Come In Here?

I have things to do, places to go
And people to see, getting ready
To go out really frustrates me

I lose my focus easily going from room
To room trying to remember –
Why did I come in here?

Glasses, keys, cell phone, I
Have to look for these things
Before I can even leave home

Why did I come in here? Is my
New catch phrase; it seems
I say it more and more these days

Losing and misplacing this or that
I refuse to accept that I have a bad case
Of I can't remember s**t

Why did I come in here?
Strikes fear in young and old alike
But I will not give in to my mind
Changing like the wind
I will fight this fickle change all
The way to the end

Legacy

I want to leave a legacy behind and
Tell the story I acquired over time

A story that can only be mine
Is my legacy to leave behind

I leave memories of my past, for my
Daughter to see and
I pray she will be proud of me

I leave a trail of love for my husband
Who stuck with me

I leave love letters for my mom and dad

I leave laughter and joy for my true friends that
Loved and supported me through thick and thin

This book is my legacy for all to know
I lived life to the fullest and I want to
Show, that it wasn't for nothing and
I will live on, in my rhymes and books
To a back drop of my favorite songs

About the Author

Photograph by Darryl Young
Hairstyle by Kim Best

Cynthia Young was born and raised in Detroit, Michigan and later moved to California where she resides today. Young continues to evolve as an author and is currently working on her next book.

"Cynthology A Collection of Rhymes Book III - Shades of Cyn" is Young's fourth book and third in the Cynthology Collection. It continues to show her growth as a writer and poet. This book shares more of her insights into real life situations, with humor and sexy story lines. Her rhymes appeal to audiences from eighteen to eighty.

"Cynthology A Collection of Rhymes" and *"Cynthology A Collection of Rhymes Book II - Electrified"* are Young's second and third books. She expresses her view on life through unedited original contemporary, relatable rhymes with twists, turns and unexpected endings.

"Memoirs of a Caregiver" is her first book. She shares her experiences of twelve years as a long distance caregiver for four family members stricken with Alzheimer's disease.

A portion of the proceeds from this book is donated to the Alzheimer's Association.

Printed in the United States
By Bookmasters